Jacey's Beautiful Difference

Illustrated by:
Green Graphics

Written by:
Melanie C. Christmas

Title of the Book: Jacey's Beautiful Difference

Author: Melanie C. Christmas

Illustrator: Green Graphics

Publisher: Craft Works Publishing

Copyright © 2025 by Melanie C. Christmas

All rights reserved. No part of this book may be reproduced, distributed, or transmitted in any form or by any means, including photocopying, recording, or other electronic or mechanical methods, without the prior written permission of the publisher, except in the case of brief quotations embodied in critical reviews and certain other noncommercial uses permitted by copyright law.

ISBN: 979-8-89704-865-6

Printed in the United States of America

Dedication

To all the little Black girls discovering the beauty of their true selves: May you always see the unique sparkle in your reflection, feel the unwavering strength in your heart, and believe in the boundless magic of your dreams. You are perfect, just the way you are, and the world is brighter because of you.

Once upon a time in a small town in Georgia lived a black girl named Jacey. Jacey was a lively, charming, and adventurous seven-year-old who had just moved with her parents to Colorado. They settled into a lovely house on a quiet street, with snow-capped mountains easily visible from their doorstep.

Jacey was full of excitement about the new setting but also felt nervous about starting her new school. The school was in a predominantly white neighborhood, unlike her old school in Georgia where most of her friends looked like her. She missed them dearly and wished they were here with her.

In the mornings, Jacey would wake up early, get dressed, and have breakfast with her parents. Her mother would help style her hair into beautiful braids or puffs before she headed off to school. At school, she'd spend the day learning new things, playing at recess, and making new friends, including a little girl named Sara.

Sara was fair-skinned with long, straight hair that swished when she moved. She was always kind to Jacey and complimented her on the things she didn't like about herself—like how different she looked from everyone else or how she spoke differently.

As time passed in their new home, Jacey began feeling unhappy about the differences between herself and her classmates. She wished to have straight hair like Sara's instead of her curly, kinky coils. She longed for skin that wasn't as dark as hers because it made her stand out among the other kids.

One sunny afternoon, while looking at herself in the mirror, Jacey noticed something magical about herself—when under sunlight, her skin radiated a beautifully golden glow that none of her classmates possessed! And as for her hair? Oh! The styles she could create were endless—from braids to afros to puffs!

The next day at school during show and tell, Jacey stood up and shared her newfound appreciation for her hair and complexion. She explained how her hair was versatile and fun—she could create all these different styles that Sara or other classmates could not. She showed off her radiant skin, expressing how it glows under the sun, making her feel proud and unique.

18

Everyone, especially Sara, clapped and cheered for Jacey. From that moment forward, Jacey was happy just the way God made her—unique, radiant, and beautiful. She realized that having features different from others did not mean she was less than them; it only meant she was uniquely special in her own way.

And so, Jacey learned a valuable lesson—to love herself and embrace the beauty of her hair texture and skin color. Her differences did not make her strange; they made her special. And being special is a beautiful thing indeed! Every night before bed, Jacey looked into the mirror with a smile on her face and gratitude in her heart—happy to be exactly who she was.

From then on, Jacey continued to inspire everyone around her with self-love and acceptance. And as for Sara? Well, they became best friends forever—two unique individuals who learned to celebrate their differences together! They lived happily ever after in their lively little community!

The End!

Mirror Me Activity

What do you see when you look in the mirror?

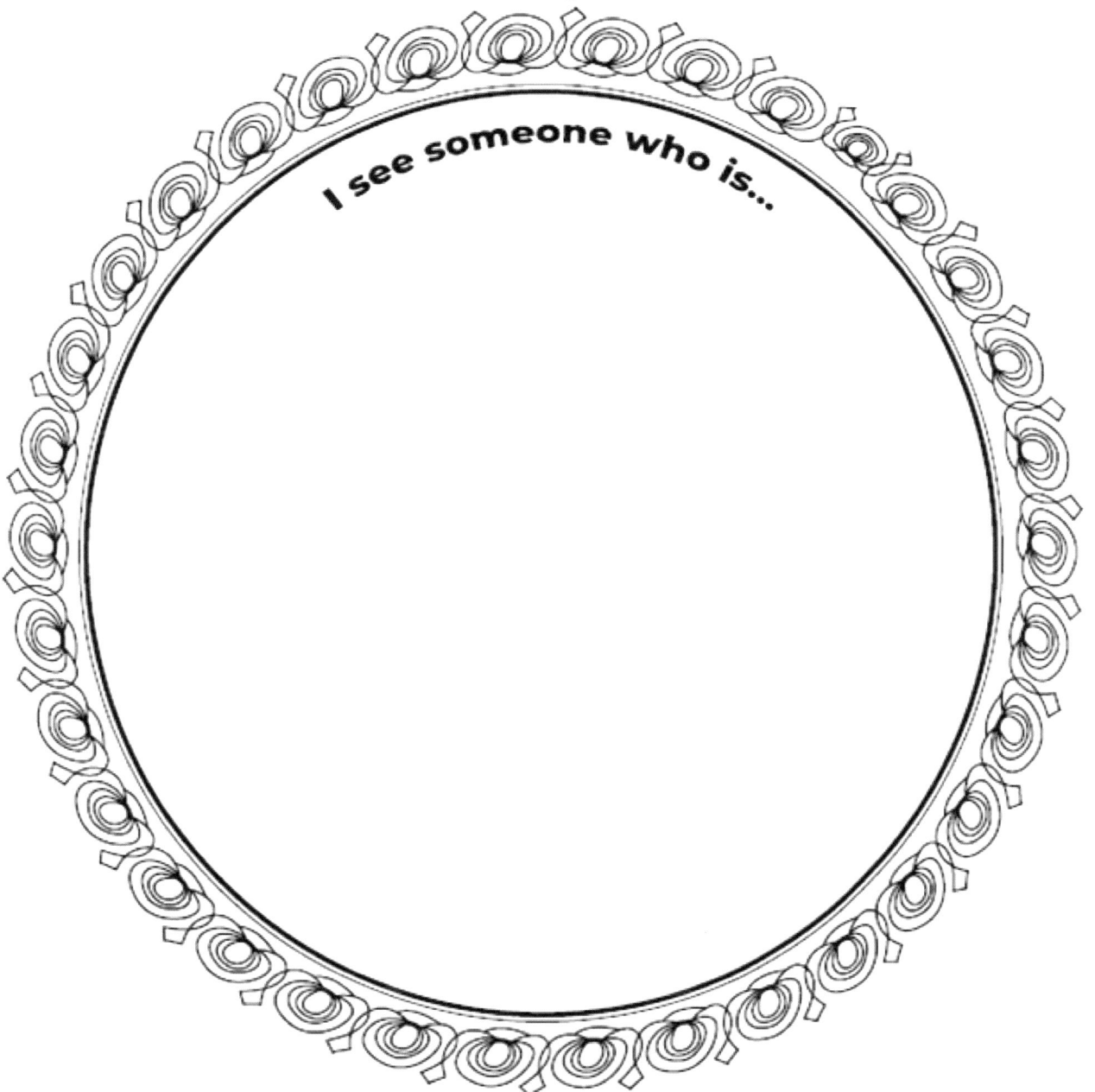

www.ingramcontent.com/pod-product-compliance
Ingram Content Group UK Ltd.
Pitfield, Milton Keynes, MK11 3LW, UK
UKRC040338240426
12049UKWH00017B/167